MAN FOOD

Fire Ant Books

MAN FOOD
Recipes from the Iron Trade

SLOSS FURNACES NATIONAL HISTORIC LANDMARK

FOREWORD BY KAREN R. UTZ

The University of Alabama Press • Tuscaloosa

We thank Bill Thorpe and Paige Wainwright for their contributions.

The University of Alabama Press
Tuscaloosa, Alabama 35487-0380
Copyright © 2007
Sloss Furnaces National Historic Landmark
All rights reserved
Manufactured in the United States of America
Designer: Michele Myatt Quinn
Typeface: ACaslon

The paper on which this book is printed meets the minimum requirements
of American National Standard for Information Sciences-Permanence of
Paper for Printed Library Materials, ANSI Z39.48-1984.

Library of Congress Cataloging-in-Publication Data

Man food : recipes from the iron trade, Sloss Furnaces National Historic
Landmark / foreword by Karen R. Utz.
    p.   cm.
"Fire Ant books."
Includes index.
ISBN-13: 978-0-8173-5451-0 (pbk. : alk. paper)
ISBN-10: 0-8173-5451-4 (alk. paper)
    1. Cookery, American. 2. Foundry workers—United States. I. Utz,
Karen R. II. Sloss Furnace Association. III. Pig iron rough notes.
    TX715.M265 2007
    641.5973—dc22   2007007311

Contents

Foreword

Following the Civil War, Alabama began to shift away from the dominance of agriculture. In 1871 prominent Alabamians formed the city of Birmingham with the express purpose of exploiting the mineral resources of north-central Alabama, where every ingredient necessary to produce iron could be found within a thirty-mile radius.

One of these men was James Withers Sloss, who had brought the L&N Railroad into Jones Valley in 1871, transforming Birmingham from a squalid jumble of tents, shanties, and boxcars into a thriving community. Anxious to tap the rich mineral areas surrounding Birmingham, Sloss and his associates acquired 30,000 acres and formed the Pratt Coal and Coke Company, which quickly became the largest mining enterprise in the district. Blast furnaces for processing the iron ore mined by Pratt soon sprang up all over Jefferson County, and pig iron production rapidly became big business in northern Alabama. By the 1880s, Birmingham was booming and due to its rapid growth had earned the nickname the "Magic City." A local newspaper stated that "this magic little city of ours has no peer in the rapidity of its growth."

As Birmingham flourished, so did James Sloss. He retired in 1886 and sold the company to financiers who guided it through a period of rapid expansion. The company reorganized in 1899 as Sloss-Sheffield Steel and Iron, although it would never make steel. With the acquisition of furnaces and extensive mineral lands in northern Alabama, Sloss-Sheffield had become the second largest producer of pig iron in the world by World War I.

In the late 1920s, under Birmingham-born president Hugh Morrow, Sloss-Sheffield completely rebuilt its blast furnaces and modernized its methods to reduce costs and increase production. Because of these improvements, Sloss-Sheffield was able to survive the Great Depression and made valuable contributions to the war effort in World War II. It went on to earn the highest profits of its history in the late 1940s and early 1950s.

Sloss-Sheffield's path to economic success was assisted by a marketing venture introduced in the late 1920s. The company began a small magazine known as *Pig-Iron Rough Notes*, a name based on the saying "rough as pig iron," with about 600 subscribers. Less than a decade later, the magazine was being mailed to almost 5,000 readers. Despite its small size, *Rough Notes* became one of Sloss-Sheffield's greatest contributions to the foundry trade, playing an educational as well as a technical role. *Rough Notes* was introduced at a time when Sloss was updating its furnace practice. Morrow, well aware that foundrymen were suspicious of change, created the magazine not only for promotional purposes, but also to show foundries that change was both beneficial and productive. Magazine editor Russell Hunt (Sloss-Sheffield secretary-treasurer) combined the company's increasingly modern scientific image with an emphasis on time-honored, old-fashioned virtues. Sloss-Sheffield, he stated, "was a corporation with a soul, deeply valuing its customers and strongly committed to prompt, personalized service." The company appointed a chemist, W. O. McMahon, as a full-time representative to visit foundries and help solve technical problems. McMahon was described by Hunt as "having as much actual experience in melting iron as any man in Alabama and will be happy to come to your plant for a day or a week, as the circumstances may demand." To emphasize that McMahon and other Sloss representatives were not afraid of "soiling their hands or clothes," Hunt coined the term "Shirt Sleeve Service."

Hunt saw the primary mission of *Pig Iron Rough Notes* as showing foundrymen that it was in their best interest to buy Sloss-Sheffield products. The magazine carried special features to promote up-to-date foundry practices and current scientific discoveries affecting the trade. Richard Moldenke, a scientist and engineer, contributed frequently to the magazine and provided readers with a wealth of scientific insight and information. Moldenke and other experts provided a body of industrial and scientific literature that had a significant impact on the developing American foundry business.

Realizing that foundrymen would appreciate free advertising and seeing their company's name in print, Hunt devoted articles in every issue to a leading entrepreneur, facility, or community predominantly associated with the foundry trade. An early issue featured the life story of Joseph Lodge, an immigrant orphan who became a leading soil pipe and hollowware manufacture in Chattanooga. Another article contained a history of the Maytag Company, which used cast iron in its washing machines. Hunt compared founder Frederick L. Maytag's contributions to the American household to those of Henry Ford to the automobile industry. In 1946, following a trip to a Chinese foundry, metallurgist E. K. Smith wrote of his experience in an article entitled "Chung Kuo Sheng T'ien" (Chinese Cast Iron). "With keen sympathy for his sufferings, and admiration for his accomplishments, I look for a great future for the foundryman of China. I remember him as courteous, unhurried, unworried, likeable, and always cheerful."

Referring to cast iron as the "Metal Eternal" and elaborating on its role throughout history, Hunt assured customers that Sloss-Sheffield's primary mission was "catering to foundrymen." Even before the 1941 attack on Pearl Harbor, *Pig Iron Rough Notes* was highlighting the importance of cast iron to national defense and stated that Sloss-Sheffield "would be ready for any and all impending hostilities." When the U.S. entered World War II, a series of articles showed how the foundry industry was preparing for victory, and to show the contributions that cast iron was making to the war effort, Hunt devoted an issue to the role women were playing in foundries.

Although subscribers and readers appreciated the wide array of foundry topics offered in *Rough Notes*, it was a human interest facet that became a mainstay of the publication. Recognizing the passion foundrymen had for the "great outdoors," Hunt encouraged his readers to submit their hunting and fishing experiences, as well as the recipes that resulted from these outdoor excursions. The enthusiastic response to Hunt's request resulted in a feature entitled "Gentlemen Cooks." "Gentlemen Cooks" (with its customary byline, "Cookery is become an art, a noble science; cooks are gentlemen!") became a standard element and offered recipes ranging from Tennessee Squirrel Stew to Catfish Chowder. A 1948 issue highlighted Muskrat Stew and recommended that the first thing one must do in preparing this delicacy was to "skin, decapitate and remove entrails, being careful not to puncture musk gland." The recipe ended with the note that "corn sticks or hush puppies are very good served with this dish."

These unusual yet fun and entertaining recipes speak to simpler times when family recipes and traditions were treasured and passed on to friends and fellow workers. But the recipes in "Gentlemen Cooks" also reveal something else: they show a personal side to an industry often associated with harsh metals, chemicals, and fiery blast furnaces; a gentler side that was seldom seen by those outside the foundry and iron industry.

We hope that you will enjoy them also.

Karen R. Utz, Curator

Sloss Furnaces National Historic Site

MAN FOOD

1
Sloss on the Food Front
Russell Hunt

Produce more foods of the right kinds.

Conserve food, avoid waste.

Play fair in buying food—share it cheerfully and fairly through rationing.

Place the war first and expect to adjust to wartime and postwar conditions.

Napoleon's famous observation that "an army travels on its belly" is just as true today as it was back in the early 1800s. Recently a smart Washington official said, "Steel and TNT are the sinews of war, but Food is its blood stream." So, any way we may view the war question it will be found that *food* is the very first consideration. It is no wonder, therefore, that our government is taking such an active interest in food production with its innumerable ramifications. Food is easily the most widely discussed question in the country, aside from the actual battlefronts.

One now refers to the *mass* production of food, for it has become a highly skilled and even technical business. The growing of large food and feed crops is requiring more and more mechanical tools and implements. Were it not for these modern aids, the farmers would be utterly unable to furnish the needed foodstuffs for war and civilian needs. The growing of foods has become a very important section of big business.

Our readers may well wonder what connection Sloss pig iron could possibly have with food. True enough, every well-balanced diet includes iron, but not exactly in the form of pigs! Yet, upon

close examination, it will be found that Sloss iron is at this very moment doing yeoman's service in the production and processing of many of our chief foods. Sounds ridiculous, doesn't it, but true nevertheless for the production of food involves many factors and much hard work. To particularize: preparation of the land, planting of the seeds, cultivation, pest control, harvesting, processing, transportation, warehousing, and distribution. We are not overlooking the preparation and serving of food, but that is such a long story it will have to wait until another time. Each of these operations not only requires labor from uncounted hands, but also implements of many kinds—from the simplest to some of the most efficient and intricate machines the ingenuity of man has ever built.

Even our almost casual examination of the mechanics of food

production reveals an astonishingly large variety of implements and devices constructed in part with gray-iron castings made from Sloss iron: plows, tractors, pulverizers, harrows, spreaders, planters, grain drills, fertilizer distributors, sprayers, cultivators, grinding plates, corn huskers, food choppers, meat grinders, cane mills, dough mixers, peanut pickers, potato peelers, juice extractors, bread slicing machines, farm wagons, warehousing trucks, farm power units—to mention just a few out of hundreds of food production appliances being made by Sloss customers. These foundries are surely participating in this vital part of the war effort—the production and distribution of food.

In exploring the interesting possibility of finding the actual end uses of Sloss iron, the food question was found to be so vast that mention of only a few of our customers—one here and there—could be made in this number of "Rough Notes." Our purpose has been to try and present the little known fact that pig iron—generally considered as a crude raw material—plays an intimate and important role in the many complexes of our daily lives. It has been an interesting task to attempt to relate many foundry products with the Food Front, and we hope our efforts will be informative to our readers.

While Sloss iron may not be good enough to eat, it is plenty good enough to help do a very important job along the entire Food Front.

2
Hollowware By "Lodge"

Sloss furnishes iron to a number of stove foundries operating special hollowware departments, also to Lodge Manufacturing Company, one of the few concerns making cast-iron hollowware exclusively.

Lodge has devoted nearly 30 years to developing and improving kitchen utensils and enjoys a nationwide distribution. Sloss uses a special burden of brown ores for making pig iron for this class of work and we verily believe that it will not only make a smoother casting but one that will take the highest polish of any made in America.

Cast-iron hollowware is staging a great comeback. For a while many substitutes appeared on the market, but in recent years, the unequalled qualities of cast iron have been more and more appreciated. The stores are still full of lightweight and somewhat flimsy makeshift skillets, pots, etc., perhaps utilized chiefly by young couples living over their garages and within a gill-of-gas distance from

This modern hollowware made by Lodge Manufacturing Company, South Pittsburg, Tenn., with Sloss' Noala brand of pig iron is known far and wide to American housewives ("Queens" in their own kitchens) as "jewels" in the preparation of "the way to a man's heart."

the delicatessen. But for real folks, those millions who "live at home and board at the same place," there's only one choice in cooking utensils and that is cast-iron hollowware.

3
Bean Hole Beans

Women continue to invade almost every sphere of men's activities. In the Editor's travels in selling pig iron he has run across more than one woman foundryman (or is it foundrywoman?) and at least one woman blacksmith, and, boy, did she swing a wicked hammer! Now this invasion has gone far enough—why can't we men try something in a supposedly woman's field? The quotation about gentlemen cooks came from a poem of 1600 A.D. Men, is it not time to regain our early standing?

Are you following us? Gentlemen are finding more leisure time these days, and what would be more delightful than learning to become proficient in preparing one or more special dishes, which could be served at informal stag or mixed parties, preferably out-of-doors and at camps? A happy time indeed awaits such a one.

As a starter we offer:

Recipe For Bean Hole Beans
The bean hole pot should be roughly 18" long, 15" wide and 15" deep. Size does not greatly matter, but it must be deep enough so that the bean pot will be buried under four or five inches of soil. Next, secure a dozen or more stones or brick about the size of your two fists. Maintain a good fire in the bean hole for two or three hours, gradually putting in the stones or brick. These are

necessary in all new bean holes: after use, the ground is baked and dried out, so the stones are not absolutely necessary in the holes—but are always a help in maintaining an even heat and are particularly needed when the soil is sandy or moist.

For four persons—take a pound preferably of great northern navy beans and let them soak while the bean hole is being heated. The soaking is not necessary, but it helps slightly to improve the final results. Just before the bean hole is ready, drain off the water in which the beans have soaked and bring them to a boil in fresh water. When they come to a boil add a teaspoon of soda, let them boil in the soda water for ten minutes, and drain. A cast-iron bean pot with cover is preferred. One half pound of salt pork cut in half-inch cubes, one large onion cut in squares, ¼ cup of molasses, ¼ cup of sugar, one level teaspoonful of salt, and one tablespoonful of mustard completes the recipe.

The fire will now have died down to embers. Take these and the hot stones out of the hole—set the bean pot on the bottom of the hole. Now arrange a row of hot stones all around the pot a distance of two to four inches from the pot. The stones must not touch the pot. Scratch the embers and soil from the pile made when digging the hole to fill in between the pot and the hot

Cast-Iron Bean Pot

stones. Make this layer of soil and embers deep enough to cover the stones. Now repeat another row of stones and more hot embers until the bean pot is entirely covered. Finally, cover the hole with a good, deep layer of soil. Tramp it down. If made at night, the beans will come out steaming in the morning, every bean whole, yet soft enough to melt in the mouth and deliciously flavored. From five to ten hours is the necessary length of time required to cook.

Supplied by Frank Hamilton of Gadsden, Alabama, a perfect host and gentleman cook. Bean hole beans is Mr. Hamilton's gastronomic specialty and if directions are followed, a dish "fit for the gods" will be the result.

4
A Foolproof Way to Cook Fish

The echoes from our last recipe (Bean Hole Beans—Autumn 1939) are most gratifying and we believe we struck a popular chord. Men are more and more finding their reaction in the great outdoors where to be able to cook a real man's dish is an art indeed. We now offer:

A Foolproof Way to Cook Fish

This recipe is contributed by a busy New Yorker whose business interests embrace many fields; in addition, he is an ardent farmer (or shall we say agriculturist?), an enthusiastic camper, an excellent fisherman, and one who cooks his own fish. Here is his story:

There are many good meat cooks, some good fish cooks, but few who can cook both. Also, I have heard it said that there are ways and ways and ways of cooking fish but some are better than others.

To my way of thinking I have settled down to almost a standard method that, with slight modifications, will apply to almost any kind of fish. Particularly is this simple method good for outdoor and camp cooking, where time is essential on canoe trips or destinations in view with time-out for lunch along a stream or on the shore of a lake with a fresh mess of trout or bass in hand. In fact, the sooner a fish is cooked and eaten after being caught, the better its flavor.

First, in preparing the fish, such as trout, bass, perch, and similar fish, always scale in preference to removing bones and skinning such as is often done when fish are plentiful and when guides are handy with a knife. All flavor is then retained.

Second, thoroughly dredge or sprinkle fish with flour or cornmeal, whichever is available and preferred as to taste.

Third, the old fashioned cast-iron skillet or frying pan is best. To my mind, there is no substitute for a cast-iron pan or griddle or pot for stewing.

Fourth, melt enough butter in pan, to a light brown color, just beginning to smoke, to the depth of about $\frac{3}{16}$ to $\frac{1}{4}$ of an inch; next add one equal quantity or slightly more of good cooking olive oil. Any food oil will do but the cooking oil is somewhat cheaper. I buy it in convenient pint or quart tin containers with a replaceable tight cap.

When this mixture is heated to the smoking point, place the fish in it, preferably flat and not touching each other. They will reach a brown color on the bottom side very quickly, and just as soon as this occurs and there is a substantial crust, turn the fish over carefully, still keeping a very hot fire.

When each side is thoroughly browned add two or three slices of lemon and the juice of a whole lemon, lowering the heat and putting a cover over the pan. Also at this stage I like to season with salt and black pepper. The cover will throw the heat down on the fish so that the thicker portions and the meat around the bones will be cooked slowly without overcooking the outside and still keep the moisture in so dryness will not result. I find the easiest and surest way of determining when the fish is properly cooked is to make a short slit with a sharp knife in the thickest part of the fish—examination will disclose if thoroughly done.

When serving, put plenty of the butter, oil and lemon mixture over each piece of fish.

The same method is even more desirable in cooking fish steaks, such as red fish, king fish, grouper, tuna, halibut, etc., because if properly followed the flesh will be moist completely through, even in steaks up to 1½ inches thick, but of course a great deal more time must be used after the browning period to allow the slower heat to soak through and thoroughly cook.

I have tried combinations other than butter and oil but never with the same success. The oil seems to soak in when cooking and the butter does the browning.

5
Brunswick Stew for Ten

Our campaign to convert foundrymen into cooks goes merrily on. "Every last foundryman an outdoor-cook." With more time for recreation—camping, picnicking, etc., etc., let it not be said that we men know not how to use our hands.

An Alabama Barbecue is a thing of beauty, a joy forever,—but the *pièce de résistance* is the Brunswick Stew, its ever-preset companion. Your editor is a barbecue-hound, and along with many, thinks that, if possible, the stew is more delicious than the barbecued meats. Our recipe for this delectable dish comes from none other than our food fiend, Hon. J. P. Phillips, of Birmingham, affectionately known to thousands over the South as "Papa Jack." If we should attempt to give you an account of Mr. Phillips' many accomplishments, we are sure we would never outline the recipe! We also regret that limited space precludes including a history of this world-famous collation.

Brunswick Stew
(For ten persons)

3 pounds of fat, fresh brisket of beef, finely ground; place in a cast-iron pot, with 6 or 7 pints of water; 1 tablespoon vinegar, 1 tablespoon salt; boil for one hour; this gives you the stock.

Put 1 teaspoon baking soda in a teacup of boiling water; and stir up well. Pour into stock, stirring well. Skim off foam.

Place 1 tablespoon celery-seed in a small muslin bag; put in a teacup of boiling water to make a strong tea and pour into stock.

2 lbs. of Irish potatoes—peel and slice thin

½ lb. onions—sliced fine

2 lbs. canned tomatoes

1½ lbs. canned corn

1 teacup canned okra

Put in pot.

SEASONING

Stir well in pot:

½ teaspoon sugar

½ teaspoon salt

½ teaspoon white pepper

Boil slowly for one hour, stirring regularly. If stew is not thick, thoroughly mix one cup flour with cold water, put in pot, and stir well.

When this concoction is ready, call the editor so that he can share the rich reward with you.

6
Italian Spaghetti

With the camping season in full bloom, it is estimated that literally tens of thousands of men are adding to their pleasure by cooking out in the open.

Many people have a real desire for good Italian Spaghetti, and since there are so few restaurants where the genuine article can be obtained, it is felt that the following recipe will be of special interest

Cast-Iron Pot for Brunswick Stew

to "gentlemen cooks." It is an excellent dish during cold weather and likewise makes an excellent meal for camping and fishing trips, provided the sauce is prepared in advance (at home).

Seemingly sensing this desire, our good friend, C. E. Bales, has sent in the recipe appearing below. Mr. Bales is noted for his famous spaghetti suppers and, when not engaged in playing the role of host to his many friends, may be found at the Ironton Fire Brick Company's big plant at Ironton, Ohio, where he serves as Vice President in Charge of Manufacture. Mr. Bales states that the sauce is the most important item—something of a "tail-wagging-the-dog" affair maybe!

Italian Spaghetti

To prepare the sauce, grind ½ pound smoked ham and ½ pound beefsteak through a meat grinder. Finely chop 2 large onions and three cloves of garlic. Brown the ground meat, onions, and garlic in bacon grease or olive oil in an iron skillet. Stir frequently, until the meat is fairly well done—requires about 10 minutes.

Transfer this to an iron pot and add 2 small cans of Italian tomato paste (not tomato pulp), 1 large can of tomatoes, ⅛ pound butter, 2 pints water, ½ teaspoon salt, ½ teaspoon ground red pepper, and 1 tablespoon mixed spices placed in a small muslin bag during the cooking of the sauce. Cover the iron pot and allow to simmer for four hours, stirring frequently.

In cooking the spaghetti, the long, unbroken pieces should be placed in boiling, salted water, and allowed to boil for about eight minutes. Do not cook too long or the spaghetti will become soft and soggy. Remove the spaghetti from the pot with a large, perforated dipper, or pour into a large colander, and drain off the water.

Place the spaghetti in large soup plates, cover with the sauce, and sprinkle the top with grated Parmisello Italian cheese.

Come and get it!

7
Genuine "Chow Club" Clam Chowder

Camping has become so popular that it now knows no season. Fall and winter weekends in the woods are quite the thing, and we know of no recreation more wholesome. But back to our recipes.

We are indebted to Walter Bullard, "a metallurgist with a personality," of the United Shoe Machinery Corporation, Beverly, Mass., for a fine recipe for Clam Chowder. He secured it from a Scottish sailor, and we give it to you exactly as received:

Genuine "Chow Club" Clam Chowder

Take 1½ pecks good, clean clams in shell. Put in iron kettle, with water enough to cover soup plate. Boil until clams open up. Remove and strain off liquor through cloth. Clean kettle and then put clam liquor back.

Now slice up ½ pound salt pork into an iron frying pan, frying out all fat until pork is browned. Add to the fat 4 or 5 medium onions, chopped up, and cook until onions are soft and mellow.

Meanwhile, dice up about 12 to 15 medium size potatoes; put these into clam liquor, adding enough water to cover potatoes.

When they begin to boil, add onions and pork-fat and the clams which have been shucked and skinned. Cook until potatoes are done, remove from fire, and after about 15 minutes add 2 quarts good milk into which a dozen Marblehead crackers have been soaked. Now, add a good piece of butter and put back on fire, but do not allow it to boil. Add salt and pepper to taste.

Just right for a party of seven or eight gentlemen. If made five or six hours before ready to use, will greatly improve flavor; simply heat when ready to use.

8
Shrimp a la Creole

While our mouths are watering, it will be a good time to include our favorite Shrimp a la Creole dish. This comes direct from the French Quarter, New Orleans, brought up by Ralph Silver, well-known advertising counselor of Birmingham:

4 lbs. of shrimp

½ small button garlic, sliced

4 green bell peppers (optional)

1 can Italian tomato paste

¾ cup salad oil

1 bunch shallots, or 1 large

3 heaping tablespoons flour

onion

Salt and pepper to taste

Clean shrimp (remove shell and black thread) and boil for five minutes. Heat oil in an iron skillet until it begins to smoke. Make a roux by adding the flour to the oil and stirring until it browns. Add onions, brown slightly, then add shrimp. Add salt and pepper to taste. Stir around until each shrimp is coated and none of the roux or onions stick to the skillet. Here add tomato paste, green pepper, and garlic, stirring around continuously for 15 minutes more over a moderately low flame.

All tomato paste should now be sticking to the shrimp. Push a few shrimp aside and add one cup hot water in bottom of skillet. Turn flame as low as possible, cooking 15 minutes longer without stirring—then stir again, add 3 or 4 cups hot water as before, and cook over low flame, without stirring, for an hour longer. Do not cover the skillet. Serve hot.

The chef says that when cooking most seafood, it is necessary to cook them very gently. Once water is added, never allow the mixture to boil hard, or the flavor will be ruined.

9
On Cooking Steaks

One of our reader-gentlemen-cooks has made a timely suggestion to the culinary department. He says, "Let's pass up the 'spoon vittles,' and get right down to the meat." In other words, he would like an idea on cooking a steak; and come to think of it—in a man's estimation, there's nothing like a good steak!

It has been said that the buffalo hunters used the one perfect method of cooking steaks. When hungry, the hunter would shoot a nice fat buffalo, cut out three steaks, each about two inches thick, and place them right in the coals; when done, the middle steak would have absorbed the juices of the other two which were thrown away, and a dish suitable for the gods resulted. However, in these days, when we poor city fellows have to pay 75¢ to $1.00 per pound for a good sirloin, it is impracticable to follow the hunter.

Our good friend, Stanley Bobbitt, has stepped into the breach with a fine recipe on steaks. Mr. Bobbitt is not only a gentleman cook, but a fine gentleman in every other way. The hospitality of the Bobbitt home (and backyard) is quite as well-known as that of his city, Anniston, Alabama. Friend Bobbitt knows both his onions and his steaks!

STEAK ON THE HOOF

Mr. Bobbitt says that a good steak must be started in the cattle-country. First, you select a healthy yearling; one with a kind but lazy expression. See that this yearling is never made to run and be sure that it is put in the best location for watering and eating with as little effort as possible. During the last six months of this period of preparation of your steak, it is best to keep this live meat in a corral with plenty of prize corn to eat. See that it never becomes angry, as there is nothing that hurts a steak like gallbladder secretion from fright or anger. When this live meat reaches the stage that it waddles instead of walking, then the first important step has been handled.

Next, put this beef in a livestock fair, where it will be sure to win a blue ribbon. There is nothing like blue-ribbon prize beef, because, after all, nine-tenths of the taste of steaks is in the mind anyway. As to the slaughtering, storage, and other details, Armour, Wilson, Cudahy, and others have always been willing to look out for this. By all means, have your steaks cut from the sirloin; and they should not be less than two inches thick.

Broiled Steak

Broil the steak over charcoal—in a cast-iron utensil—rare or medium-rare. Charcoal should be burned down to red coals, with all of the volatile burned out. Seal the juices of the steak in by quickly cooking it on one side. As you turn the steak, rub it with garlic. The steak should not need much more cooking after it has been rubbed with the garlic . . . about twenty minutes in all.

Cover the cooked steaks with butter and sprinklings of salt and pepper to taste. Hit over the head with a belaying pin the first man who tries to change the flavor with catsup, meat sauce, mushrooms, or onions. Ask your guests as they arrive how they prefer their steaks. If anyone says "well-done," just tell them to come back Monday, for lunch, when the cook serves Sunday's roast as hash.

10
"The Sportsman"

Recently, the Editor ran across, in a hardware store, an ingenious portable cast-iron camp stove. It seems to be "tops" over anything we have ever seen in this line. It is ideal for "Gentlemen Cooks," for the backyard or camps: fits nicely into the car trunk and fills a long-felt want. Of course, we were thrilled to find that "The Sportsman" is manufactured by old Sloss friends, The Atlanta Stove Works, of Atlanta, Georgia, having been fully patented. The stove is versatile to the nth degree . . . adaptable for fast frying, both slow and fast broiling, and smothering. It's a "honey"; made of Sloss iron; very compact, strong, and light. We simply couldn't resist running a cut!

"The Sportsman"

11

Lentils and Sausage with Fresh Green Corn

With the return of spring, T. B. M.'s thoughts turn lightly to the great outdoors; a surprising number, in planning outings, arrange to do a little man-cooking, as well.

For these two recipes, we are indebted to a kinsman of the editor, the Hon. Nat Rogan, collector of Internal Revenue at Los Angeles. When he is not checking over the income tax returns of Gable, Garbo, and other celebrities, he can be found, more than likely, pulling a supper party at his Chula Vista ranch. He is a past-master in the art—truly a gentleman cook. Naturally, he uses cast-iron utensils exclusively in his cooking, for in this way true flavors are retained.

Lentils and Sausage

Look over 2 cups of lentils to be certain there are not tiny pebbles among them. Wash well and put in a large pan. Cover well with water; add 1 or 2 onions and let simmer until tender. In a large iron skillet, melt a ¼ pound butter; add 1 large clove of garlic, finely minced (or more if desired!), and a generous amount of chopped parsley. Add the lentils, with their liquor, to the mixture and simmer until reduced to the moisture desired; do not have too dry.

Fry patties of sausage-meat* to serve with the lentils. Sourdough French bread and claret wine complete this delicious meal.

Fresh Green Corn

Take 12 ears of corn, splitting the kernels straight down each ear; cut the remaining kernels off, then scrape the cob for the milk left. Add 1 cup finely chopped chives; if chives are not available, use tops of young green onions, finely chopped. Salt and pepper to taste; add butter, and half-cream-and-milk, or milk depending upon the richness desired. Mix well and put in a buttered cast-iron skillet. Sprinkle top with Parmesan cheese—preferably fresh-grated rather than the canned-grated kind. Place in a moderately hot oven and as soon as the cheese is melted, serve.

Corn not to be boiled.

*If sausage is not available, use garlic frankfurters.

12
Concerning Salads . . .

Not so long ago, all salads were considered effeminate—or, rather, for serving only to the gentler sex. But times do change! Nowadays, gentlemen are not sissies simply because they like—even demand—a green salad at luncheon. The trend is actually toward more salads and fewer desserts.

Salads cover a large territory; one can be "thrown together" from almost anything edible. No special skill is necessary to bring forth a worthy dish.

Success of the Salad Lies in the Salad Dressing . . .
An Alabama gourmet tells us that the glory of the salad is the dressing; the secret of a good salad dressing lies almost entirely in the proper blending, or mixing, of the several ingredients. We are pleased to offer his recipe for:

"Prolifico Salad Dressing"

1 cup olive oil (Wesson's will do in a pinch)
½ cup vinegar (apple, or any standard type will suffice)
Some parsley, chopped fine
1 onion, small, and grated so fine it blends with the mixture
1 egg, beaten well
Salt to taste
Pepper to taste
6 small cloves of garlic, chopped fine (3 cloves of average size are sufficient, generally)
2 level teaspoons mustard (prepared, or dry made into paste)

(Ed. Note: We have been told the above ingredients make the most unusual salad dressing that has been introduced in this section of the country for many years. Its name is reported to have come from the fact that it is approximately the same dressing enjoyed by the Dionnes!)

These ingredients, beaten together, make a smooth dressing for lettuce, or other forms of leafy or fresh-vegetable salads. Double the ingredients if more than one pint is wanted; it will keep in the icebox for several days, and is better the second or third day than when freshly made. After that, it all depends . . . on whether you or the garlic remains the stronger. And—if you have guessed—this is a dressing that should be used sparingly. However, do not be surprised to see the guests sopping up the drippings after eating their lettuce . . . or whatever you put underneath the dressing.

Would anyone care for dessert?

13
Pan Fried Fish

We are indebted to a good friend and sportsman for this old and tried method of cooking fish which, if followed, will result in the true flavor being retained.

Pan Fried Fish

Select a medium-sized fish; leave the head on, but gills should be cut out. The body will hold together better when the head is not removed.

Use 3 or 4 tablespoons of pure olive oil with a little butter added. The olive oil will keep the flesh juicy white. The butter will brown the outside. Roll the fish in corn meal. The meal flavor blends nicely with the flesh of the fish. A deep cast-iron frying pan is best for cast-iron utensils help preserve the fish flavor. This is true of all foods when cooked in cast-iron vessels.

Fish, unlike steak, should be cooked slowly, preferably over a good bed of coals. When cooked this way the backbone will separate whole and complete on the plate.

A perforated lid should be kept on the pan during cooking so that the moisture from the fish can escape as steam.

Now, dear reader, if you have followed us to this point, you should now be ready to go out forthwith and catch some fish for the pan! Well, if you use the Cafeteria Bait system, catching fish will merely be a detail.

CAFETERIA BAIT

When it comes down to the matter of lures, the average fisherman is somewhat like a youth we once met trolling on a lake. As we approached, we watched it weave as he reeled it in. He had five or six plugs, tandem spinners, and bucktails fastened together on a wire coat hanger.

"Son, what do you call that?"

"That," he answered, "is my cafeteria bait."

"Cafeteria bait? That's the funniest named lure yet. Why do you call it that?"

"Well, you see, it's like this," he grinned. "I just drag it past the fish, and they pick out what they want."

14
Hobo Stew

The interest of foundrymen in both indoor and outdoor cooking shows no signs of abating and the Editor is having loads of fun in running across "gentlemen cooks" on almost every business trip. The latest one to be discovered is none other than J. J. (Jack) Chandler, plant manager of the Somerville Iron Works, Chattanooga, Tenn. Jack is perhaps personally known to more molders and foundry foremen in the southeast than any other foundry executive. His counsel and advice on iron melting and other branches of foundry operation is constantly sought by scads of people, but it is not so generally known that, in addition to his many accomplishments, he is an expert cook as well.

In his younger days, in a burst of patriotism, he enlisted in Uncle Sam's Navy and landed with both feet in the galley of a big battleship. He showed so much natural ability and aptitude for peeling spuds and washing dishes that the chief officer (Jack being willing thereto) arranged instantly to put him through a course at a real cooking school, from which he emerged as a full-fledged cook in his own right.

Jack recalls that his ship had a complement of 1100 tars and he and his assistants were really kept busy rolling out the chow. Every Sunday morning hot cakes were on the menu and that meant 3300 flapjacks! After serving his "stretch" in the navy, Jack went into foundry work as a molder, starting at a stove shop in Rome, Ga. Well, he molded "up and down, all around the town" and in many another shop and town, eventually going to Chattanooga where he helped in planning the large Somerville plants, remaining as fore-man, then superintendent, and later as plant manager, a position he still holds with credit. His son, Ralph, also joined the navy, not as a cook, but after graduating with honor at the U.S. Naval Academy at Annapolis in the class of 1940 and is now in service on the high seas. The other son, John, is a student at the University of Tennessee.

Our original purpose was not to give a history of this ex-hobo molder, but rather to put our readers "in the know" with Jack's famous "Hobo Stew," a potent dish for real hungry men, simple to prepare and guaranteed to satisfy.

Hobo Stew

> 2 lbs. flank stew meat
> 1 #2 can tomatoes
> 1 #2 can carrots
> 1 #1 can vegetable soup
> 1 # 1 can June peas
> 1 #1 can pork & beans
> 2 lbs. Irish potatoes, diced into 1" cubes
> Boil the meat until well done; then add ¼ lb. of butter, and all

of the vegetables except the potatoes. Stir constantly so that the ingredients will not stick to the pot, and cook 15 minutes. Then add the potatoes, and cook about 20 minutes longer. Season with salt and pepper to taste.

Note: Important that a cast-iron pot be used. Serve with pumpernickel.

The above amount should serve at least ten hoboes.

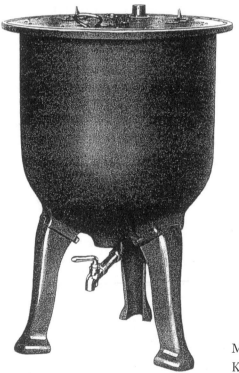

Majestic "Chow" Pressure Kettle

15
Hush Puppies and Fried Fish after the Florida Manner

(Editor's Note: We are pleased and honored to be able to present, with the author's permission, recipes from "Cross Creek" a current best seller in Florida life by Marjorie Kinnan Rawlings, who also wrote "The Yearling" and other intensely interesting Florida stories.)

Hush Puppies and Fried Fish after the Florida Manner

FROM THE BOOK "CROSS CREEK"

There are elevated Floridians who turn up their noses at hush puppies, but any huntsman would not exchange a plate of them for crêpes suzette. They are made and served only in camp or when one is frying fresh-caught fish informally at home with the returned fishermen clustered comfortably in the kitchen while the cook works.

First, you fry your pristine fish, boned and filleted, rolled in fine cornmeal and salt, and dropped into sizzling fat. You lift out the fish, golden-brown, and lay them on pie plates close to the campfire. While they have been frying, you have stirred up your mixture: fine cornmeal, salt, a little soda or baking powder, an egg or two or three if the camp be affluent, and, if you want hush puppies de résistance, finely chopped raw onion. You make the mixture dry and firm. You pat it into little cakes or croquettes between your hands and drop the patties into the smoking deep fat in which the fish have been fried. They brown quickly to the color of winter oak leaves, and you must be sure to have your coffee and any other trifles ready, for when hush puppies are brown, your meal is ready. . . . Do they sound impossible? I assure you that under the open sky they are so succulent that you do not care whether you have the rest of your dinner.

CAST-IRON CAMP SKILLET

Writer Marjorie Kinnan Rawlings has the following to say about cast-iron cooking vessels and this alone would qualify her as an authority on the culinary art: "Cast Iron is so superior for cooking utensils to our modern aluminum that I not only cannot grieve for the pioneer hardship of cooking in iron over the hearth, but shall retire if necessary to the backyard with my two Dutch Ovens, turning over all my aluminum cookers for airplanes with a secret delight."

16
German Favorites

Leberkloes und Sauerkraut
(Liver Dumplings and Sauerkraut)

To 1 lb. of raw calf's liver ground with a small piece of suet, add 2 strips of cubed bacon and ½ finely cut onion browned in butter. Also add 2 eggs, salt, pepper, nutmeg, a pinch of cloves, and finely cut parsley. To this add enough rolled cracker crumbs to make firm balls.

Cast-iron Camp Skillet

Try 1 liver dumpling in boiling water. If not firm enough, add more cracker crumbs. Dip hands in cold water and roll liver into balls. Drop into boiling salt water and let simmer 30 minutes. Skim out of water and pour melted butter and finely cut onions over same. Serve with sauerkraut and mashed potatoes. This recipe will serve a family of four.

Linsen Suppe and Bratwurst
(Lentil Soup and Pork Sausage)

Boil 1 lb. lentils. Drain off water and start to boil again in warm water. When lentils are nearly soft, add one cubed raw potato, celery, and salt.

Short time before serving put sausage into soup and heat thoroughly. Melt 3 tablespoons of butter, blend into this 2 tablespoons of flour. Stir until smooth and add this to soup. This soup can also be cooked with beef broth.

Chef's Suggestion: this recipe is calculated to satisfy four persons. However, for pig iron and foundry individuals the quantities are to be at least doubled. It is further suggested that there be provided one or more kegs of Michelob. In due time this will inevitably promote the singing of "Ach du lieber Augustine" and "Schnitzelbank," followed by "Hail, Hail, the Gang's All Here," winding up with "Sweet Adeline."

17
Tea

BREWING TEA—CHINESE FASHION

Tea is easily the best-known beverage in the world. It is a source of comfort and strength to untold millions every day. The origin of tea as a beverage is shrouded in antiquity; although there is some Chinese record of the plant as early as 2750 B.C., it is not generally thought that tea was served as a beverage until about 700 A.D. Spanish traders introduced it to Europe in 1528.

It seems strange that with tea being universally liked, few people, comparatively speaking, really know how to brew tea properly. An Englishman told the Editor once that Americans did not understand the art at all, and he may be right.

It is a real pleasure to be able to present a charming Chinese lady's recipe: It is good for we were graciously served in her home the best tea we ever drank. Here it is in English and also in her native Chinese:

置熱水茶壺中約十分鐘俟壺熱後倾去熱水放入每一茶杯沸水一茶匙、茶葉跑後倾沸水於茶葉上緊闭壺蓋經四十五分鐘之護醇葉之味唐乃才入茶四此見浮葉王加另搅俟其下沉但倾茶於杯叶不致古仿四硪

After the Chinese

How to Make Tea

THE SAME THING IN ENGLISH

Warm the teapot by filling it with hot water and leave it in the pot for about ten minutes—then empty out the water and put into the pre-warmed teapot a teaspoonful of tea leaves for every cup of boiling water.

Pour into the teapot and over the tea leaves boiling water, then allow it to brew for three to ten minutes (depending on strength desired) to secure the full flavor of the tea. Stir the tea leaves and allow a minute or two for the leaves to settle before serving.

(Note: It is always preferable to brew tea in an unglazed earthenware pot.)

"I give you the sovereign drink of pleasure and of health in cups that cheer but not inebriate."

18
Cooking Gear

FRUIT GRINDER AND PRESS

The R. W. Whitehurst Manufacturing Corporation of Norfolk, Virginia, is the leading producer of fruit grinders and presses, also cider mills, their "Boss" line being in demand from coast to coast. Now that the entire country has become fruit conscious, Whitehurst is busier than ever. They also make a complete line of agricultural implements too numerous to mention here. The Company, founded in 1879, is under the active management of Chas. H. Hix, Jr., as president. Their foundry uses Sloss iron in all castings.

Fruit Grinder and Press

Cast-Iron Ware by Lodge Adds Character to the Kitchen

Under our civilization, food would be of little use if cooking utensils were not available. Cast-iron ware has been the mainstay in cooking foods for centuries and remains the best media today. There is something indescribable about the flavor of food prepared in the old cast-iron skillet or pot that the new-fangled methods can't begin to touch. Cast-iron cooking utensils may not be so appropriate for folks living over garages and around the corner from a delicatessen but for real people who "live at home and board at the same place" they are necessary.

Cast-Iron Ware by Lodge Adds Character to the Kitchen

Lodge Manufacturing Company of South Pittsburg, Tennessee, is one of the foremost producers of Cast-Iron cooking utensils. Their products are marketed in all forty-eight states and in many foreign countries. Sloss pig iron is exclusive here.

A Juice Extractor is a Necessity in Every Kitchen
Vitamin-laden Florida orange juice is fast becoming the nation's No. 1 breakfast fruit and a reliable and efficient juice extractor is a must on every housewife's list. Such a contrivance, shown on the next page, is by Hamilton Beach Company of Racine, Wisconsin. This company also makes a dandy drink mixer and many other useful things used in preparing food.

All castings are from the foundries of the Western Foundry Company of Chicago where Sloss iron has been in their mixes for many years. The Western Company is one of the largest gray-iron foundry operators in this country.

Rookie's Respite
Whatizit? Washing machine?
NO! A streamlined potato peeler.
One of these machines can peel a bushel a minute without waste,

A Juice Extractor Is a
Necessity in Every Kitchen

Rookie's Respite

flats or bruises, provided one can find the spuds. Just imagine how this peeler lifts the morale of the inductee!

This amazing machine not only peels potatoes but many other vegetables such as beets, sweet potatoes, turnips, carrots, horseradish, etc., many times faster than by hand. Made by Reynolds Electric Company, Chicago, it is standard equipment for the army, navy, canneries, large restaurants, and others.

All castings by National Sewing Machine Co., of Belvedere, Illinois, which uses Sloss pig iron in its mix regularly. National is now making castings for numerous machines necessary to the war effort, while in peacetimes their fine sewing machines are sold all over the world. Sloss iron is in the foundry mix.

FRENCHERETTE CUTTER

French fried potatoes are as American as "ham 'n' eggs"—both being rather scarce just now. No wonder that some smart fellow arose to invent this useful cutter, which will handle a whole peck of potatoes in ten minutes. A great boon to army cooks—or any kind of cooks.

These items are from the Chicago Hardware Foundry Company's North Chicago foundry. This company manufactures a large variety of articles including restaurant equipment, kitchen accessories, furniture hardware, metal specialties, etc. At present they are supplying mess room equipment for all types of naval vessels. They are making a real contribution in the sanitary and efficient preparation and serving of foods, and in other directions. Sloss has been a part of their mix for many years.

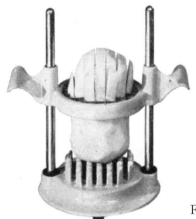

Frencherette Cutter

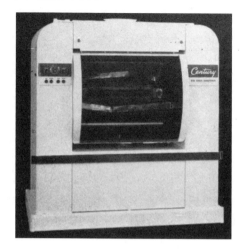

"Let Them Eat Cake" (And Bread, Too). Century 2 BBL. Dough Conditioner

"LET THEM EAT CAKE!" (AND BREAD TOO)
Century 2 BBL. Dough Conditioner

Mass production of bread has been greatly simplified by this Century high speed dough mixer, a product of The Century Machine Company of Cincinnati.

All castings used are from the foundry of Standard Casting Company, also of Cincinnati. Standard has long been a Sloss customer and is busily engaged furnishing quality castings for machines needed on the food and other fronts.

ENTERPRISE MEAT CUTTER
Capacity 2,000 Lbs. Hour

This Enterprise chopper (with some of its sisters) could quickly prepare the "makin's" for enough hamburgers to satisfy our soldiers down to the most recent inductees. Enterprise makes a large line of choppers, sausage grinders, stuffing equipment, coffee mills, and other food processing devices that are in worldwide demand.

Enterprise Meat Chopper

Castings by Alabama Foundry Company in Birmingham. This splendid production foundry specializes in many classes of high-grade light gray-iron castings. A 100% Sloss iron melter.

19
A Recipe from Australia

Just as we were about to go to press we received from one of our good friends and readers, Mr. D. M. McDonald, secretary, Metal Trades Employers' Association, in far away Sydney, Australia, an intriguing recipe which he states is very popular in the greatest sheep-growing country on the globe. Now, if we can "point" up some lamb, our satisfaction will be complete:

Lamb En Casserole
2½ lbs. loin of lamb

¼ lb. (½ cup) butter

¼ lb. (½ cup) rice

2 egg yolks

1 pint (2 cups) good gravy

Salt and pepper

1 blade mace

A little grated nutmeg

Half roast the loin of lamb and cut it into steaks. Boil the rice in boiling salted water for ten minutes, drain it, and add to it the gravy with the nutmeg and the mace: cook slowly until the rice begins to thicken, remove from the fire, stir in the butter, and when melted, add the yolks of eggs well beaten; butter a casserole well, sprinkle the steaks with salt and pepper, dip them in melted butter, and lay them in the buttered dish; pour over the gravy that comes from them, add the rice and simmer for half an hour.

20
Alabama Camp Coffee

Café au Lait—Café noir—Café ala Crème—Creole Coffee—Vienna Coffee—Plain Everyday Coffee—who can say that this method or that method makes the best coffee? Coffee is the world's great beverage for men of both high and low degree and in between, all the way up or down the human scale.

While the coffee tree was known to Abyssinia as early as the sixth century A.D., it appears to have been very carefully guarded for there is no record of the plant in other countries until the ninth century when its cultivation seemed to have spread into Arabia, and later into other Eastern lands. Coffee as a beverage was not introduced into Europe, by way of Venice, until the year 1645 and is therefore, comparatively speaking, rather new to the Western World. The first coffee houses in Venice were a great success, rapidly spreading to England and all over the civilized world.

Coffee being the favorite mealtime drink for at least 99.44% of all fishermen, huntsmen, and general sportsmen everywhere, the Editor thought it very strange that there should be such a continual controversy raging over the proper way to make coffee. True enough, all sportsmen seem to drink the coffee served up in camp, on a boat, or elsewhere but seldom indeed is open praise offered the cook for having made good coffee. Many times, complaints have been voiced about the poor coffee—at a discreet distance though. Our curiosity over this raging controversy finally won and we asked that great American Sportsman, Charles S. "Mudhorse" Martin,* the man who has all the answers, to give us the true and final word. He, as always, had the answer which we gladly offer for the benefit of the unknowing:

Rinse pot; add a cup of cold water for each cup of coffee to be made and 1 cup, for the pot. Put in a tablespoonful of coffee grounds for each cup desired. Let the pot boil over for one moment, snatch it off the fire, but leave near enough that the coffee will keep hot until served.

*Sportsman Martin, when not out at his private lake and fish farm, or on the golf links, or down on the Gulf deep-sea angling, may be found at the M & H Valve & Fittings Company, Anniston, Alabama, where he serves as president—with notable success.

21
One-Dish-Meal Cooking

There is so much talk nowadays among culinary experts, so called, about one-dish-meal and en casserole cooking that one might think that something new under the sun is being cooked up. But, is this system really new? We think not, and to prove the point we are giving our readers a very old and excellent Southern recipe for a complete meal in one pot. It is supplied by our friend David Evans, of Chicago who sold Sloss foundry iron throughout the middle-West for years and years and possibly would have been selling it yet if he hadn't become rich in the steel foundry business as president and owner of the Chicago Steel Foundry Company.

Although Dave was but a lad when he left South Carolina, he never forgot his boyhood home, including the many world-famous dishes of that section. We know his contribution to "Gentlemen Cooks" will be as widely appreciated as the dish is in Charleston, Savannah, Mobile, New Orleans, and other coastal cities.

Jambalayah (Jumbi-li)
    1 to 1½ cups boiled or baked ham, diced
    1 cup boiled rice
    1 ½ cups stewed tomatoes
    1 large onion
    1 green pepper
    1 stalk celery
    Seasoning to taste, but remember the ham is salty
    Add the first three ingredients and cook for ten minutes. Then add the onion, green pepper, and celery, each one being chopped fine. Turn into a baking dish and cover with buttered crumbs and bake until top is browned. Serve very hot. Sufficient for four.

In Charleston, S.C., they use chicken or veal instead of ham, but I prefer ham as it gives more flavor and character to the dish. When cooked, this dish should not be too dry, more like a rather thin stew. It is a complete meal.

Brunswick Stew
(Another One-Dish Meal)
There is no standard recipe for Brunswick Stew. The story of its origin, as told to me by a native some fifty years ago is: A party of hunters were camped in Brunswick County, Virginia. They set out from camp one morning and during their absence the cook ran afoul of the liquor and went to sleep. The afternoon was well along when he woke up and, knowing that the party would soon be coming in ravenous for food, he hastily put a pot on the fire and proceeded to dump in all the cold leftovers he could find: rabbit, chicken, navy beans—almost anything handy. The stew had just reached a boil when in came the hunters. As always, hunger is the finest sauce in the world, so they enjoyed the dish and named it Brunswick Stew. It is still a good way to clean out the icebox and get rid of leftovers.

22
Hunter's Coffee

Coffee is the favorite mealtime beverage of perhaps half of the world's population and yet strangely enough such a controversy exists today among coffee drinkers over the best method of preparing it that one rarely finds two people who are in agreement on this point.

Assuming that many of our readers are either active hunters, campers, and/or fisherman or expect to be some day, and with coffee the No. 1 "must" on any list, we have reached up into British Columbia, that famed big-game paradise, for a hunter's coffee recipe to end all coffee recipes for outdoor sportsmen. Our thanks must go to William Deans of Vancouver, British Columbia, for this. Mr. Deans is both "Gentleman Cook" and scholar, as well as an excellent foundryman.

Hunter's Coffee

2 cups ground coffee

3 eggs

1 level teaspoon of salt

½ teaspoons of Coleman's Mustard

Put 5 quarts of boiling water into a 2-gallon coffee pot, throw in the other ingredients (crack the eggs and throw all in).

Boil briskly for 3 or 4 minutes, then douse with 1 pint cold water to settle the grounds.

Let pot stand near the fire but don't let it simmer or again boil.

This gives 16 cups of the very best—and a cup measure to an outdoor man is ½ a pint.

This should give campers a hearty drink indeed!

23
Cabbage a la Hamilton

The number of "gentlemen cooks" is increasing by leaps and bounds and, moreover, these cooks are no longer confining their culinary efforts to camping trips or to backyard barbecue facilities—they are beginning to invade the home kitchens, which from the earliest times have been the *sanctum sanctorum* of housewives and out of bounds for all men. Perhaps, this will serve to compensate in a measure for the wholesale invasion of men's domain by the weaker sex. Our observation is that men are not so fussy in preparing delectable dishes and, generally, use the plainest and simplest materials. For example, our good friend, Frank Hamilton, well known industrialist of Gadsden and Anniston, Alabama, has a recipe for cooking cabbage that is unbeatable. While this vegetable is as old as time itself and wholesome as well, no woman would serve cooked cabbage to company. Just the same, men love it!

Cabbage A La Hamilton

(Never boil your cabbage in water)

Select a nice green cabbage; peel and quarter six ripe tomatoes (two big cans if fresh ones are not available). Cut the meat from six pork chops in pieces about the size of a postage stamp. Fry the pork real brown and put aside. Cut two medium onions and fry them in the pork grease until half done.

Cook the tomatoes and onions in an iron pot until they come to a boil. Now, you are ready to cut the cabbage. Use a sharp knife and cut it in thin strings, about like shoe strings. Put the cabbage and pork in the pot with the onions and tomatoes and let boil for ten minutes. Keep lid on tight. Take four cloves of garlic and cut very, very fine, also a spray of parsley and a sprig of thyme—add these to the pot and cook for ten more minutes—not longer; if cooked too long it will be ruined. Serve with boiled rice or boiled Irish potatoes.

Sounds good, doesn't it?

24
Sloss Ladle-Mixed Foundry Pig Iron

MACHINE CAST

All three brands are machine cast. "Sloss" and "Clifton" irons are made in Birmingham, using, as a base, red ore mined locally at Sloss mines plus a scientific blending of special brown ores from the district.

"Noala" iron is made in Birmingham also, with red ore as a base, but using a much larger percentage of brown ores mined in the world-famous Muscle Shoals District of North Alabama. "Noala" has been known to foundrymen for over 35 years as the best stove plate pig iron in America. When mixed and melted properly it makes better heat-resisting castings and takes enamel perfectly.

SLOSS
Ladle-Mixed Foundry Pig Iron

As Uniform as "Peas in a Pod"
UNIFORM IN SIZE AND IN ANALYSIS

Brand	Silicon	Sulphur	Phosphorus	Manganese
"Sloss"	1.25—3.00	.05 or less	.80— .90	.50— .75
"Clifton"	1.25—3.00	.05 or less	.70— .80	.60— .75
"Noala"	1.25—3.00	.05 or less	.85— .90	.60— .75

Sloss Ladle-Mixed Foundry Pig Iron— "As Uniform as 'Peas in a Pod' "

In mining its own ores, Sloss is enabled to burden its finances with ores of such uniform analyses that regular and uniform furnace operation is ensured. This, in turn, insures a high grade and uniform iron from each Sloss furnace at all times.

Ladle Mixed

All brands of Sloss Pig Iron have the additional and exclusive advantage of being thoroughly mixed in a specially designed 125-ton mixing ladle, as the molten iron discharges from the blast furnace. This exclusive Sloss feature results in every pig of each cast being absolutely uniform in chemical analysis. It is the uniformity of Sloss Pig Iron that keeps foundry casting losses down to a minimum.

25
Outdoor Cookery Comes Into Flower

Thousands of years have passed since man conceived the spit on which to mount his meat for roasting and a crank with which to turn it. The records of past centuries are dotted with the small yet vastly important contributions that have made up our present-day methods of cooking. Man's progress has been painfully slow and the art of cooking has been no exception.

No matter how many conveniences are at hand in the modern kitchen, it is astonishing how many people enjoy cooking out-of-doors.

During the last few years this instinctive urge has been responsible for the thousands of outside fireplaces erected along our highways and in our public parks to which we flock at every opportunity. For those who wish the thrill of outdoor cooking within the privacy

Grillmaster
Barbecue Irons

of their own property, a wide variety of fireplaces is available. They range from the least expensive three-wall chimneyless type of our public parks to the pretentious masterpieces of the art found on many private estates.

But whether the construction be modest or ornate, one universal fault condemns them all—the cook's inability to control the heat. Burned steaks, ash-flecked eggs, and scorched potatoes have no place on the menu of the successful outdoor meal. This real deterrent to successful outdoor cooking has been eliminated entirely by an ingenious idea, the brain-child of a Texan known all over that great state as its premier foundryman. We refer to Mr. E. H. Trick, shop superintendent of the San Antonio plant of Alamo Iron Works. Mr. Trick's barbecue grill provides absolute control of the all-important rate of cooking—the first and only device ever made for this purpose, simplicity itself and foolproof.

Texas, perhaps, has more outdoor cookery enthusiasts than any state—not even excepting California—and the city of San Antonio, seemingly, is headquarters for this great American pastime. It was perfectly natural, therefore, that Mr. Trick should find in this environment a perfect setting in which to develop and perfect his Grillmaster Barbecue Irons. Mr. Trick is positively a benefactor to gentlemen cooks!

At our request, Mr. Trick has sent us some good Texas recipes which we gladly publish below:

Santone Barbecued Chicken

Select a young, tender chicken of about 1¼ pounds. Dress as for roasting. Split down center of back. Flatten. Wipe carefully. Rub with salt and pepper and brush with melted butter. Place on Grillmaster and lower close to fire and sear uniformly. Lift grill to medium-rate cooking position. Brush with barbecue sauce (recipe given below), turn frequently until cooked tender. Set grill just above cooking range to hold piping hot till served.

Barbecue Sauce

¼ pound of butter; ½ cup catsup; 1 tablespoonful Worcestershire sauce; 3 tablespoons lemon juice or vinegar; ½ cup water; small bag mixed spices (about 1 tablespoonful). Melt butter and mix well with other ingredients. Add bag of spices and boil for 15 minutes.

Good old Texans say this sauce can't hurt any kind of meat and can be taken straight from the bottle by anybody capable of carrying a quart of Mexican tequila without reeling!

Barbecued Wieners

1½ lbs. wieners

1 medium-sized onion

2 tablespoons vinegar

2 tablespoons butter

2 tablespoons brown sugar

4 tablespoons lemon juice

1 cup catsup

3 tablespoons Worcestershire sauce

½ tablespoons prepared mustard

½ cup water

½ teaspoon celery salt

Brown onion in butter. Add all other ingredients except wienies and cook slowly for 30 minutes. Prick skins of wienies. Pour sauce over them, cover and cook slowly until heated through (about 30 minutes). If wienies are skinless there is no need of pricking them.

(Editor's Note: Grillmaster Barbecue Irons [fully protected by patents] are made entirely of cast iron, and Mr. Trick is interested in licensing foundries to manufacture and sell them in certain trade territories on a reasonable royalty basis. The Editor has known Mr. Trick very favorably for about thirty years. He is thoroughly responsible and a gentleman in every sense of the word. Foundrymen interested in cashing in on the demand for outdoor cooking facilities that is certain to come soon from estates, dude ranches, roadside inns, clubs, lodges—anybody with a backyard—everybody should write Mr. Trick promptly for complete details. He should be addressed: Mr. E. H. Trick, Route 10, Box 228, San Antonio, Texas.)

26
Catfish Chowder and Mullet Stew

Our good friend, Carl McLean of Palatka, Florida, offers a couple of honest-to-goodness Florida recipes for our "Gentlemen Cooks." These recipes are as simple as they are unusual and we feel sure they will be tried with great interest.

Carl and his attractive wife are enthusiastic fishermen. For freshwater fishing they have the world-famous St. John's River at Palatka while for salt water sport they go across the State to their lodge on the Withlacooche at Yankeetown. The hospitality of the McLeans is surely not of this world.

Catfish Chowder

2 lbs. catfish
¼ lb. salt pork (sow belly)
1 lb. onions
1 can No. 2. tomatoes
1 lb. Irish potatoes

Dice the pork and fry to a crisp; removing the cracklins. Dice the onions, put in grease, and cook until done. Add tomatoes and cook down to a semi-paste. Add potatoes and water. When potatoes are done add 2 lbs. of fish cut in small pieces and cook until done. Black pepper and salt for seasoning.

Mullet Stew

Season water with salt and black pepper, bring to boil and add four small mullet, cut into small pieces crosswise. Use enough water to about half cover the mullet. Cover boiler and keep over a medium fire until the mullet is done and has left the bone. Add datel or other hot pepper. Will serve four.

27
Tennessee Squirrel Stew

Our friend, Gus Tindell, is honoring our readers with one of his favorite recipes, which is given below. Gus is both a big game hunter and small game hunter and anyone fortunate enough to partake of his special Tennessee Squirrel Stew has something to remember always.

A wonderful setting for this traditional Tennessee stew dish is out under some giant oak or beech tree. A very fine place for this concoction is at the Tindell farm north of Chattanooga. Like the old English recipe for roast hare which calls for catching the hare, this one calls first for freshly-killed squirrels—say, an even dozen if the crowd is large. This is a modest bag for a morning hunt in many southern localities.

Tennessee Squirrel Stew
   12 squirrels
   1 dressed hen
   6 ears fresh corn
   6 tomatoes, diced
   ½ gallon tiny butterbeans
   12 fresh potatoes, diced
   12 onions, diced
   2 red peppers

2 green peppers

12 pods okra

Salt and pepper

Cut the dressed squirrels into small chunks and put into an iron pot with enough water to cover. Stew for about 2 hours. Cut the hen into small pieces and add the now-tender squirrels. Continue to stew and when the meat begins to fall apart put in the vegetables. Continue cooking until vegetables are done. Salt and pepper to taste. (In case fresh vegetables are not available, use the equivalent from cans).

The above should serve from 12 to 20 people, depending upon the degree to which the several appetites have been whetted by the preliminaries.

28
Brunswick Stew and Spanish Rice

As already mentioned, Mr. H. Maddox has a yen for camping, likewise for camp cooking in which he is quite skilled. One of the really big events of the year for the Maddox clan is the annual camping trip which Mr. Maddox heads up and always includes the entire family with all the in-laws, grandchildren—everybody. The party comprises quite a caravan and makes straight for some nature charmspot; it may be deep in some Florida hammock or some forest in Georgia or even high in the mountains. What a wonderful way to relax and enjoy one's family!

While there are always willing and capable hands to attend to the meal preparation on these camps, Mr. Maddox personally superintends this very important department, and we are glad to give our readers a couple of his favorite recipes often used on these outings. Incidentally, these are equally as delicious when cooked in the home kitchen.

Brunswick Stew

1 lb. ground beef
1 cup butter beans
1 small onion chopped fine
1 cup corn (fresh or canned)
¼ cup dehydrated onions
1 cup canned tomatoes
Salt to taste
1 tablespoon hot sauce

Add onion to beef and season with salt and red hot sauce. Boil down and add beans, corn, and tomatoes, then boil until thick. Be sure to use an iron pot. Serves 6 to 8.

Spanish Rice

1 cup rice
¼ lb. bacon
2 cups water
1 green pepper chopped
1 teaspoon salt
2 cups canned tomatoes
¼ cup onions chopped
½ cup water
1½ teaspoons hot sauce

Cook rice in 2 cups boiling salted water 15 minutes. Cut bacon into small pieces and fry with chopped pepper and onion. When browned add tomatoes, ½ cup warm water and hot sauce. Drain rice and add to other mixture. Simmer on top of fire for 40 minutes, stirring occasionally to prevent sticking.

29
Saunders Brunswick Stew

With the barbecue season in full blast, we wanted a recipe for a genuine Brunswick Stew. Fortunately, we could turn to Eddie Trigg, the genial vice president at Tredegar, for help. He has responded nobly, in fact, we really think that he has furnished a recipe to end all recipes in Brunswick Stew. As our readers may know, this delectable dish was originated in Virginia in the eighteenth century.

Brunswick Stew always supplements a real, authentic barbecue. Really, in the years that we made the Alabama-Georgia-Tennessee barbecue circuit, we heard so many gourmets express a preference for the stew, even over the barbecued meats, that we formed the opinion that here was a true case where the tail wagged the dog. It is not so bad an idea either, in these days of very high meat prices—a good stew materially cuts down the meat consumption!

Saunders Brunswick Stew
(All ingredients are per gallon, except where other ratios are noted)
  1 lb. chicken
  2 lb. tomatoes
  ¼ lb. veal shin
  1½ ears corn or equivalent in canned corn
  ¼ lb. beef shin
  1 bunch carrots (to each 4 gallons)

1½ lb. Irish potatoes
1 bunch parsley (to each 10 gallons)
1 lb. onions
1 lb. bacon (to each 10 gallons)
½ lb. dried or canned butterbeans
1 lb. butter (to each 10 gallons)
1 bunch celery (to each 5 gallons)
Add salt and pepper to suit taste.
Note: For superior flavor, cook in an iron pot or kettle.

30
Breakfast from the Jackson Kitchen

The Jacksons are not exactly on a diet, either individually or collectively, and their house is a very popular rendezvous on Sunday mornings when hot cakes are the pièce de résistance. We consider it nothing but good luck to offer our gentlemen cooks (and their ladies) a few recipes hot from the Jackson kitchen:

1. Fort Morgan Sweet Potato Griddlecakes
1 cup milk
1 cup grated raw sweet potatoes
1 cup flour
1 large egg
1 teaspoon baking powder
⅔ teaspoon salt
1 teaspoon baking powder
Add milk to the grated potato, flour, egg, salt, and baking powder. Mix well and cook on griddle. Serve piping hot.

2. Coastal Pancakes

¼ cup powdered sugar

1 tablespoon butter

1 egg

½ teaspoon salt

¾ cup milk

1 cup flour

¼ teaspoon soda

Cream sugar and butter. Sift flour, salt, soda and baking powder, and milk together; add alternately with egg.

3. Plantation Batter Cakes

2 cup cornmeal

1 cup flour

1 teaspoon sugar

1 teaspoon salt

1 teaspoon soda

1 tablespoon melted butter

1½ cup milk

1 egg broken into dry ingredients

Mix in order given to make a thin batter. Cold boiled rice can be added to replace a portion of either the flour or the cornmeal, if preferred.

4. Alabama Old-Fashioned Batter

2 cup flour finely sifted

2 cup sweet milk

2 tablespoon baking powder

3 eggs

Beat whites and yolks of eggs separately, the former to a stiff froth. Add the flour to the yolks and beat until very light. Add the sweet milk and beat well. Now add the baking powder and beat again. Then add the whites and mix all until smooth—enough to run in a slow stream.

31
Outdoor Cooking

Outdoor cooking has become a very popular sport in its own right and almost every organization can boast of several good ones. This holds good at Martin Himself Valve and Fittings Company. Our good friend, Joe Spradley, the efficient secretary there packs a wicked frying pan, dutch oven or what have you, and is supplying some of his best recipes.

Muskrat Stew*

Skin, decapitate, and remove entrails, being careful not to puncture musk gland. Cut up into 2" pieces. Place in cast-iron pot and simmer until tender, allowing 2 cups water for each cup meat, adding ½ teaspoon salt and pinch of pepper for each cup meat.

Take another cast-iron pot and heat fat (olive oil is best), allowing ¼ cup fat to each cup of meat. Add to fat one large chopped onion for each cup meat. When onion is brown, add one can tomatoes and one green pepper chopped finely. Simmer while muskrat is cooking. When muskrat is tender, pour sauce into muskrat pot. Allow to simmer for 10 minutes, stirring occasionally to prevent sticking. If mixture cooks too low, add canned tomatoes, and simmer 10 minutes for each can of tomatoes added. Serve hot directly from pot.

Corn sticks or hush puppies are very good served with this dish.

*Readers who may not have muskrats running around their front yards can easily substitute veal or lean pork with excellent results.

Hush Puppies-Alabama
Serves 8 people

    2 cups unbolted corn meal

    1 tablespoon baking powder

    1 cup flour

    1 egg

    1 teaspoon salt

    1 large onion grated fine

Sift together meal, flour, salt, and baking powder. Add whole egg and grated onion, including juice. Add cold water slowly while stirring thoroughly until mixture forms a medium stiff batter. Allow to stand for 30 minutes before cooking. Cook in deep fat in which fish have been fried. Dip tablespoonful and push with teaspoon into hot fat. They will sink and immediately rise and float, forming round or oval shape. Allow to become golden brown, remove and place on paper to drain. Caution: Never stir mixture after once mixed; to do so will destroy effects of baking powder.

This recipe is especially good with fried fish. When served with fried chicken, rabbit, or squirrel, same as above except use 2 cups flour and 1 cup meal.

Beef Stew—Hunt Style

    2 lbs. lean beef

    6 onions

    2 tablespoons flour

    6 potatoes

    2 tablespoons fat

    1 cup green peas

    2 cups water

    2 teaspoons salt

    1 can Hunt's tomato sauce

    ¼ teaspoon pepper

    ½ bay leaf

    6 carrots

    ½ teaspoon thyme

Wipe pieces of beef with damp cloth, roll in flour. Brown in fat in heavy kettle or saucepan. Add water, Hunt's tomato sauce, and seasonings. Cover tightly and cook over low heat until almost tender—about 1½ hours. Then add prepared onions, carrots, and potatoes. Cook about 30 to 45 minutes longer. Just before vegetables are tender, add the green peas. Serves six.

32
Southern Fried Chicken with Milk Gravy

Our recipe for this issue is a natural for it has been lifted right out of Hardwick's Cook Book (a copy with each gas range), and should serve as a recipe to end all recipes for fried chicken.

BEEF STEW—HUNT STYLE

2 lbs. lean beef	6 onions
2 tbsp. flour	6 potatoes
2 tbsp. fat	1 cup green peas
2 cups water	2 tsp. salt
1 can Hunt's Tomato	¼ tsp. pepper
Sauce	½ bay leaf
6 carrots	⅛ tsp. thyme

Wipe pieces of beef with damp cloth, roll in flour. Brown in fat in heavy kettle or saucepan. Add water, Hunt's Tomato Sauce, and seasonings. Cover tightly and cook over low heat until almost tender — about 1½ hours. Then add prepared onions, carrots and potatoes. Cook about 30 to 45 minutes longer. Just before vegetables are tender, add the green peas. Serves six.

Hunt-for the best

Hunt Foods, Inc., Los Angeles, California

Southern Fried Chicken

These directions are for fried chicken exactly as it has been prepared for many generations in the Deep South.

Disjoint, wash, dry, salt young chicken not over twelve weeks old. Just before frying, roll the pieces in flour. Use large iron skillet which can be tightly covered. Put ¼ lb. shortening into skillet, melt, and bring to medium heat. Lard or vegetable shortening may be used, or half of one of these and the other half bacon grease.

Put in chicken and tightly cover, adjusting burner to medium heat. Cook ten minutes, then turn chicken, replace cover on pan, and cook ten minutes longer. Then remove cover and let chicken brown, turning if necessary. Chicken should be a light, even, golden brown. Remove chicken to hot serving platter.

In putting chicken in skillet, pack it as tightly as possible but pieces should not be stacked on each other. The neck, back, and liver cook more quickly than breast and legs, so as you remove a piece or two from the skillet fit the leftover pieces in. If you are cooking more than one chicken it is better to use two skillets. Dry, fluffy rice is usually served at the same meal to be eaten with chicken milk gravy.

Milk Gravy

Pour off half the fat in which chicken has been fried, leaving half in the pan with any brown bits which may have come off the chicken while frying—this adds flavor to the gravy. Add ¼ cup flour, salt, and pepper to the fat left in the skillet. Stir flour in the grease until it is quite brown. Have ready 1 pint of half water, half milk. Pour in ¾ of this liquid to the hot fat and flour mixture. Pour rapidly, the gravy will lump if liquid is added a little at a time. Cook, stirring while it thickens, until the gravy is the consistency of cream sauce. If it is too thick, add the remainder of the milk and water mixture, and continue cooking for a minute or two until well blended. Put in gravy boat. Serve on dry rice.

33
Dinner from the Old North State

We have reached up into Mrs. Frank Dowd's kitchen card index to bring our readers some honest-to-goodness Old North State recipes—recipes that men will enjoy and which they can, without much bother, prepare upon occasion.

Pot Roast
  5 lbs. round of beef
  1 tablespoon Worcestershire sauce
  1 cup grated onions
  Salt and pepper
  1 cup grated carrots
  Cooked macaroni or broad cut noodles
  1 cup currant jelly
  1 cup hot water
  Pimento strips
  Wipe meat and sear in frying pan until well brown. Place in deep cast-iron pot with water and simmer until tender, replacing water as it cooks away. Keep tightly covered and after one hour

add seasonings. Half an hour before serving add vegetables and jelly. Place the roast on an oval platter and arrange the macaroni or noodles, pour gravy over all. Garnish with narrow strips of pimento.

34
Dinner in a Dish

Dinner in a Dish
> 1 lb. hamburger
> 1 medium onion, chopped
> 2 eggs
> 4 tablespoons shortening or butter
> 2 cups corn
> ½ cup dry bread crumbs
> 4 medium tomatoes, sliced
> 1½ tsp. salt
> 2 green peppers, chopped
> ¼ tsp. pepper

Put the shortening in an iron skillet and lightly fry the pepper and onion for three minutes. Add the meat and blend thoroughly. Add the seasoning. Remove from fire, stir in eggs, and mix well. Put one cup of corn in baking dish; then one-half the meat mixture; then a layer of sliced tomatoes; then another layer of corn, the meat mixture, and tomatoes. Cover with bread crumbs. Dot with butter and bake in a moderate oven (375ºF) for 35 minutes.

Spoon Bread
> 2 cups corn meal

2 teaspoon baking powder (with sweet milk) or ½ teaspoon soda

2 cups hot water

1 teaspoon salt

1 tablespoon lard (with buttermilk)

2 cups sweet or buttermilk

3 eggs

Let meal and hot water stand for one hour. Separate eggs. Mix all ingredients but egg whites. Add beaten egg whites last. Bake in deep pan 40 minutes.

35
Floridians Also Like Barbecues

Recently I had the good fortune to attend a large private barbecue in Florida and having first-hand knowledge of many of our readers' interest in such matters, I believe a brief resume of the method employed down here will be worthwhile.

Pits of the permanent type seem to be in favor—masonry affairs built above ground, the popular dimensions are three feet wide and seven feet long with one end left open for firing. The question of size is for each individual to determine for himself. An iron grid (or heavy wire) is placed across the top to hold the meat. Also, a tin hood or cover is placed above the grid, being raised or lowered by a pulley arrangement and is a very useful innovation as we shall see.

A fire is built of hickory logs about ten hours before serving time and four hours is allowed to build up a deep bed of coals. In no case should there be any flame to scorch the meat; coals must be used only in the cooking process so an efficient pit has a small auxiliary one at the side where logs are kept burning. As these produce coals they are used to supplement the main fire. This is an important detail.

Six hours before the feast (for feast it will be) the meat, which has been well salted, is placed on the grill and the hood is kept about three feet above it until thirty minutes before serving. This keeps the smoke above the meat to flavor it and also keeps out the rain (you know how it usually rains at outdoor parties).

A barbecue sauce of salt, black and red pepper, Tabasco, sage, vinegar and ground bay leaves is whipped up (my host seemed to mix these by guess and by gosh). Then the cooking meat is swabbed every thirty minutes with the sauce which is applied by a cloth wrapped around a stick. This swabbing continues throughout the cooking period. At the halfway point the tempo is stepped up to every twenty minutes. As a final touch, the hood is lowered for the last half hour of cooking to a point just above the meat. This browns the meat thoroughly and flavors it more.

Dear readers, you have my word for it, this is barbecuing in the grand manner.

36
Grandma and—

The stove on the next page was made in 1849 and used by four generations of the same family for a total of 90 years, and then it was bought by the original manufacturer. It is still in good usable condition.

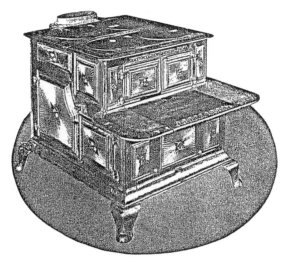

Old Prairie State Cook Stove made by Comstock-
Castle Stove Company, Quincy, Illinois.

37
Shrimp Cuba

If we were asked what food was most preferred by tourists traveling
over Florida we would unhesitatingly answer "shrimp" and add that
it was also preferred by the natives. With fresh shrimp (or frozen)
now available throughout the land, there is no reason why inlanders
cannot enjoy this delicious crustacean as well and as often as those
residing near the sea.

One of our new Floridian friends has given us a new recipe which
he brought up from Cuba. We hasten to pass it on to you for it's a
lulu!

Shrimp Cuba

    1 cup green peppers

    ½ cup mushrooms

    1 medium onion

    2 cups tomatoes

    1½ cups cooked rice

    2 tablespoons oil

    2 cups cooked shrimp (salt and pepper)

Chop up peppers, onion, shrimp, and mushrooms. Sauté the peppers and onion in oil until soft. Add the shrimp, rice, mushrooms, tomatoes, salt, and pepper. Mix it all up well, cover with bread crumbs, and bake until the top browns. It's a real treat when done right.

38
"It Sticks to the Ribs"

At long last many distinctly Southern foods are coming into their own for famous dietitians are now recommending them for their high vitamin content. Among the items being especially mentioned are okra, turnip greens, collard greens, and blackeye peas, all of which have been standbys in every Southern kitchen for generations. We were astonished to see in a recent issue of *Life* an editorial headed: "It Sticks To The Ribs" referring to that old Southern favorite, okra!

We once heard a famous physician say that the slaves with a diet of turnip greens, salt pork, waterground corn meal, rice, okra, and buttermilk were better nourished than present day city dwellers. If the many victims of malnutrition to be seen on every hand are any sign, the physician was eminently correct.

We think all of this calls for a big dish of:

Hopping John

2 cups dried blackeye peas

2 cups cooked rice

¼ lb. salt pork

2 tablespoons of margarine

Salt and pepper to taste

Soak peas overnight. Boil with pork and a little water until tender. Add cooked rice, season with salt and pepper and margarine. Cover and simmer for 15 minutes. Serves about eight.

Note: Use a cast-iron pot for best results.

39
Delicious Charcoal Broil Soy Steaks

We are indebted to Randolph M. Lee of the Hawaii Aeronautics Commission for the following recipe.

Delicious Charcoal Broil Soy Steaks

3 lbs. tender steaks (cut in individual servings) one-half inch in thickness

1 pint soy sauce (preferably Japanese)

1 level tablespoon chopped ginger root

1 heaping tablespoon brown sugar

1 level tablespoon chopped garlic

Combine the soy sauce, ginger root, brown sugar, and garlic; soak the steaks in the mixture for two hours; then broil the steaks over a charcoal fire.

Caution: Excessive soaking and/or cooking of steaks tend to create a salty condition. If using a high flame over the charcoal, sear the steaks only. Use proportionate measures for larger quantities. It is not advisable to prepare less than 3 lbs. of steak. The sauce may be salvaged for use again provided it is kept under refrigeration and strained to remove meat particles.

40
Beef Kabobs

We are indebted to Clyde H. Adams, chef, Dale's Cellar, Birmingham, Alabama, for the following recipe:

Beef Kabobs

Cubes of lean, tender beef on a skewer with alternating slices of onion, tomato, and green pepper.

Purchase best grade of well trimmed sirloin tip or top round of beef, cut to a thickness of at least 1 inch. Have this cut into 1 inch cubes and run through a cubing machine. Following cubing, fold the pieces to once again yield pieces approximating 1 inch cubes.

Place beef cubes alternated with slices of onion and green tomato on a stainless steel skewer. A 9-inch skewer will accommodate 5 cubes of beef and 4 each of tomato and onion. In preparing the onion do not cut through the rings but, rather, use a segment of onion similar to a segment of orange peel.

Barbecue over a low charcoal fire for 20 to 25 minutes. If hickory charcoal is not available, hickory wood chips, previously wet with water, can be placed around the edges of the fire and will yield the same result. Turn the skewer frequently and baste the meat with a good barbecue sauce alternated with melted butter. A suitable barbecue sauce can be prepared from the following recipe.

1 pint soy sauce

1 level tablespoon of ginger

1 heaping tablespoon brown sugar

1 level tablespoon chopped garlic

Jumbo shrimp when prepared in the same fashion are delicious. Remove the shell and vein from green shrimp and proceed as above.

41
Baked Beans

The following is a time-tested recipe for baked beans from French Canada.

Soak, overnight, in cold water containing a pinch of soda, 4 cups of yellow eye (or other variety) beans.

Drain and place the beans in a cast-iron or earthenware pot; add boiling water until the beans are covered to a depth of one inch. Cook in an oven at 300° F. for one hour.

Add two level teaspoons of powdered mustard and a half pound or more of scalded salt pork, cut into small cubes; add one cup of molasses.

Continue cooking at 300° F. for 5 or 6 hours; add water at intervals, as required to maintain the level.

42
Chile Relleños

We are indebted to Glenn O. Perry, Arabian American Oil Company, Saudi Arabia, for the following recipe.

Chile Relleños

Take 6 large green peppers (one per person), wash thoroughly, and place in hot oven for about 10 minutes, after which the outer skin can easily be removed. Also pull out core and wash inside— then pack with cottage cheese.

Take the whites of 6 eggs—beat stiff and add 1 tablespoon flour, ½ teaspoon baking powder. Dip stuffed pepper in this for outer coating and place in hot deep fat. Dip hot grease over pepper and continue until brown all over. Place them in large, deep, dry pan.

Take 1 can tomatoes and add 2 large onions diced very fine with 2 pods of garlic, pinch of salt and 2 dashes of Tabasco sauce. Cook until onions are done. Add 1 pint of whipped cream and pour over peppers. Simmer for about 10 minutes before serving.

43
Shrimp Cocktail Sauce

This may not be the best shrimp cocktail sauce in the world, but your "would-be editor" dislikes a good percentage of the cocktail sauces served on shrimp, particularly those bordering on a mayonnaise type sauce, so has concocted one that seems to be well liked by my neighbors. In fact, it was in self-defense that the measuring of the ingredients was attempted because our neighbors were calling on me all too regularly to make this sauce for them.

The sauce is not hot to the taste, unless you spill the Tabasco, but the delayed reaction of the horseradish can be increased until the roots of the hair on your head tingle, if you desire. The writer has found that Heinz dry horseradish not only keeps well, but that it is easy to measure accurately the amount desired. The one teaspoon listed will make a rather mild horseradish flavor, and I favor a heaping spoonful.

1 teaspoon dried prepared horseradish, combined with 2 teaspoons vinegar—let this mixture stand while preparing other ingredients

½ cup catsup

½ cup chili sauce

Juice of 1½ lemons

1 teaspoon celery salt

10 drops Tabasco sauce

2 teaspoons Worcestershire sauce

Dash red pepper

⅛ teaspoon salt

Mix well and chill.

The quantities listed in this recipe will serve about twelve if you are not too liberal with the sauce, but only serves about four in my family when we put the sauce in the cocktail dish and about twenty-five or thirty shrimp on the plate.

M. L. "Lip" Carl

44

Fried Green Tomatoes

There is an art to making pig iron and frying green tomatoes. Everyone does not have the industrious skill to swing a two-man hammer. Nor can everyone take firm green tomatoes and transform them into a lip-smacking side order with greens and cornbread; or a mouth-watering summer afternoon snack while sitting on the porch.

This recipe, by J. M. Brown of Edgewater, Alabama, will satisfy four hungry customers.

Fried Green Tomatoes

    4 or 5 medium size green tomatoes

    1 cup of cornmeal or flour

    Seasoning salt—to taste

    ¾ cup vegetable oil

    1 sheet of wax paper

    10" or 12" iron skillet

Wash tomatoes thoroughly, especially if you pick them from a backyard garden. Cut tomatoes in ¼ thick slices. Lay out the sheet of wax paper. Place the cornmeal on a corner of the wax paper. Spread the slices on the remainder. Sprinkle the slices with the seasoning salt, and dip them in the cornmeal one at a time, making sure both sides are covered. At a medium temperature, heat approximately ¼ cup of oil. Place the slices in the skillet— about 7 to 8 slices at a time to avoid overcrowding. Let fry until slices are golden brown on both sides. Repeat process, adding a small amount of oil each time, until all the tomatoes slices are cooked and everyone is full.

Note: Turn tomatoes over separately, like a hamburger, to avoid a sticky collision.

Cornbread Southern Style

4 tablespoons of flour

1 cup of corn meal

1 tablespoon of baking powder

¼ teaspoon of salt

1 tablespoon of sugar

1 egg

⅔ cups of buttermilk

2 tablespoons of oil or until bottom of 8" iron skillet is covered

Preheat oven to 400 degrees. Mix dry ingredients together in the order listed above. Stir in the egg and ⅔ cups of buttermilk. Place greased skillet in oven for 2 or 3 minutes. Pour remaining oil left in skillet into the batter. Stir batter. Slowly pour batter in skillet. Place skillet in oven for 30 minutes or until golden brown. Allow bread to cook for additional 5 to 10 minutes. Then slice bread and eat with greens and sweet potatoes; syrup and butter; or by itself.

Serving: 8 slices

J. M. Brown—Edgewater, AL

Shirt Sleeve Service (sales representatives, Summer 1955)

Index of Recipes

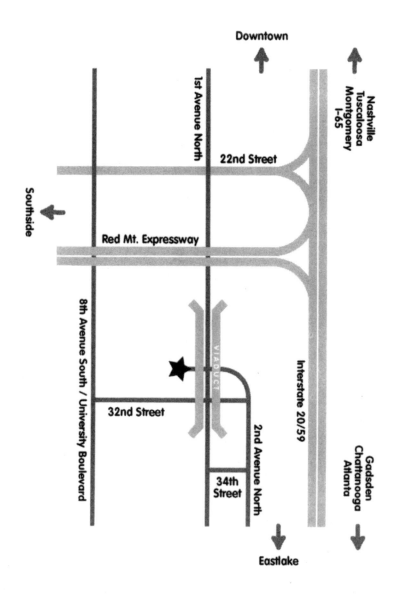

Map to Sloss Furnaces National Historic Landmark (from Sloss website)

On April 18, 1882:

Sloss Furnaces began producing iron and did not stop until ninety years later. Over the decades, Sloss Furnaces gave rise to the city of Birmingham and served as a battleground for economic, employment, and social reform. Now recognized as a National Historic Landmark, Sloss Furnaces is open to the public as a museum of industry which speaks to the contributions of the working men who labored there. With its massive furnaces, web of pipes, and tall smokestacks, it offers us a glimpse into the great industrial past of the South and our nation.